Revolution
INDOMABLE

ABHIJIT NASKAR

Revolution Indomable

Copyright © 2020 Abhijit Naskar

This is a work of non-fiction

An Amazon Publishing Company, 1st Edition, 2020

Printed in the United States of America

ISBN: 9798649610940

REVOLUTION INDOMABLE

Also by Abhijit Naskar

The Art of Neuroscience in Everything
Your Own Neuron: A Tour of Your Psychic Brain
The God Parasite: Revelation of Neuroscience
The Spirituality Engine
Love Sutra: The Neuroscientific Manual of Love
Homo: A Brief History of Consciousness
Neurosutra: The Abhijit Naskar Collection
Autobiography of God: Biopsy of A Cognitive Reality
Biopsy of Religions: Neuroanalysis towards Universal
Tolerance
Prescription: Treating India's Soul
What is Mind?
In Search of Divinity: Journey to The Kingdom of Conscience
Love, God & Neurons: Memoir of a scientist who found
himself by getting lost
The Islamophobic Civilization: Voyage of Acceptance
Neurons of Jesus: Mind of A Teacher, Spouse & Thinker
Neurons, Oxygen & Nanak
The Education Decree
Principia Humanitas
The Krishna Cancer
Rowdy Buddha: The First Sapiens
We Are All Black: A Treatise on Racism
The Bengal Tigress: A Treatise on Gender Equality
Either Civilized or Phobic: A Treatise on Homosexuality
Wise Mating: A Treatise on Monogamy
Illusion of Religion: A Treatise on Religious
Fundamentalism
The Film Testament
Human Making is Our Mission: A Treatise on Parenting
I Am The Thread: My Mission
7 Billion Gods: Humans Above All
Lord is My Sheep: Gospel of Human
Morality Absolute
A Push in Perception
Let The Poor Be Your God
Conscience over Nonsense
Saint of The Sapiens
Time to Save Medicine
Fabric of Humanity

Build Bridges not Walls: In the name of Americana
The Constitution of The United Peoples of Earth
Lives to Serve Before I Sleep
When Humans Unite: Making A World Without Borders
All For Acceptance
Monk Meets World
Mission Reality
Citizens of Peace: Beyond The Savagery of Sovereignty
Operation Justice: To Make A Society That Needs No Law
See No Gender
The Gospel of Technology
Every Generation Needs Caretakers: The Gospel of
Patriotism
Aşkanjali: The Sufi Sermon
Mad About Humans: World Maker's Almanac
When Call The People: My World My Responsibility

*This book is dedicated to all my Latinx
families across the world.*

*I cannot stop the oppressions of the past,
but I'll keep working till death,
to prevent the oppressions of the future.*

CONTENTS

1. Elixir of Service

You wanted to know how I get my ideas - I don't - my ideas get me. Just as Mozart could hear an entire symphony in his head, just as Tesla could envision an invention before it's invented, I dance with words through infinity. I and my words are not separate but one. I am my words, my words are me. Take my words and you'll have me - you'll have Naskar.

Naskar is not a he or a she, Naskar is a force - a force of unity - a force of inclusivity - a force of acceptance. But here is the important part, I am not here to entertain you or take away your miseries - I am her to make you think - I am here to walk with you while you dig deep inside your mind to discover the strength you never thought you had. However, I must make it quite clear, think ten times before you start reading me, for I am an insanity, an insanity that turns even a lifeless stone into a humanitarian force ready to sacrifice itself in the service of others.

One who has tasted the elixir of sacrifice is not satisfied by anything but the pursuit of service. One who has celebrated the festival of revolution is not appeased by anything short of self-determination. And, walking alone on the path of justice and self-determination is more honorable than walking with millions on a path of bigotry, segregation and blind loyalty. And you may set off on the path of justice and equality on your own, but you won't be alone for long, for it's human nature to follow the flame that radiates humaneness. In short, humans run towards humaneness, no matter who they come from.

Humaneness is its own religion, it is its own law, it is its own reason. In fact, all the religions, laws and reasons in the world are mere juvenile representations of humaneness - once the humans realize that humaneness in every molecule of their body, all external religions, laws and reasons will scatter and wither away.

The human whose humaneness is awake, doesn't need external archetypes of religion, law and reason to live a righteous, just and inclusive life. Footsteps of humaneness are footsteps of holiness. If you realize your humaneness, then you have realized all the religions, laws and philosophies in the world, whereas one who has studied all the religions, laws and philosophies and yet hasn't realized their own humaneness, has understood nothing.

Whether you have studied one scripture or all the publications in the world, if you don't know the value of life, all your knowledge is worthless. And unfortunately most of the human population is filled with such worthless knowledge, and that's precisely why even in this modern era of unimaginable human achievements, inhumanities still prevail. Hence, the need for revolution will never go away, so long as there is even a single trace of inhumanity among the humans.

2. Revolution Sonnet

What is revolution you ask!

Revolution is an alarm,
To wake up the sleeping population.
Revolution is a weapon,
To fight tyranny and exploitation.
Revolution is a vaccine,
To prime the society against inhumanity.
Revolution is an insanity,
To humanize the paradigm of sanity.
Revolution is a tsunami,
To wash away all that's foul and carnal.
Revolution is a tornado,
To weaken the grasp of the animal.
Whenever savages raise their fangs most
appalling,
Be not a mute witness but a revolution
sanctifying.

3. Antidote to Inhumanity

Every generation has its inhumanity, so every generation must have its revolution. The manifestation of revolution may differ based on the time and era, but the spirit and nature of it remain the same - that is, sacrifice and upliftment. Without revolution, civilization comes to halt, because with complacency arrives indifference, and with indifference comes the fall of civilization.

But here is the irony of the matter. Most humans live in complacency, hence most of them live with indifference. Unless they themselves are wronged, their sleep of indifference never breaks. Yet the society moves on - why and how you ask! It's because of those handful of individuals who ain't ready to submit to savagery, regardless of whether that savagery is faced by themselves or others in the society. Imbued with the spirit of sacrifice a handful of mad, impractical, headstrong bravehearts must stand on guard against injustice and discrimination, or else our entire humankind is bound to fade away from the face of the planet.

So, awake, arise and redeem your land from the clutches of bigots and separatists. And if you care not as to what happens to our society, then we will keep on having animals in the highest offices of our world. Savages understand only one language, that's the language of revolution. You can't reason with savages. Savages have change of heart only in movies and tv shows, not in real life. However, we must be very careful while using the term savage to refer to a person. Shortcomings do not make a person a savage. Mistakes do not make a person a savage. Savage is one who is consistent in their acts of inhumanity. So, to put it simply, consistent inhumanity is the sign of savagery.

And the only antidote to inhumanity is humanity - the humanity that lies in you. In fact, humanity of an entire people is predicated on the humanity in your veins – the humanity that flows through you the individual. Hence, your blood holds the antibodies that can protect an entire people against the sickness of inhumanity. And here is the interesting part - protecting a people against inhumanity, doesn't necessarily mean you have to leave everything and go out on the streets in protest - the revolution begins when you the individual - you the plain ordinary human being with a family, stand up to the common inhumanities you face in your daily walks of life.

The real practical revolution begins when you stand up in front of an everyday injustice and say - "no more". When enough individuals across the world stand up to such everyday injustice, no inhumanity will have the guts to raise its foul fangs. Injustice rises only in the absence of humanity. When your humanity insists that no matter what happens, you must never bow before inhumanity, either in loyalty or through indifference, your very resolve will take away the ground from beneath the feet of inhumanity.

The fate of every inhumanity is predicated on the act of humanity. Inhumanity can exist only when humanity is asleep. Wake up the humanity in you and the inhumanity around will turn powerless. Refute brutality and practice humanity. In short, the fate of inhumanity is in the hands of humanity, not the other way around. Once you realize this simple fact at the core of your being, nothing can stop the revolution born from that realization.

Revolution begins with realization. And realization can't be taught or learnt. It can only be lived. It's like being thirsty - when you are thirsty, you don't need somebody else to tell you that you are thirsty, you just feel it within. Likewise, when something is not working in your society, you must feel it in your bones, and once you do, you don't make sacrifice, sacrifice makes you - that's when the real revolution begins.

Unless the desire for sacrifice oozes out of every nerve ending in your body, there is no hope for progress and prosperity. Live long or not doesn't matter, but live with purpose, because your purpose adds meaning to not only your life, but also that of your society, nay, our society. And remember, without determination, a purpose is not different from the dreams that you have while asleep.

Let the force of determination merge with your very existence and the bearers of barbarism will tremble in fear. If you are righteous, if you are humane, if you are conscientious, why should you be afraid of the barbarians - why should you be scared at the threats of the animals! In short, if you are human - if you think, feel and act human, then it's you of whom the animals should be afraid, not the other way around.

4. Who's Human, Who's Animal

Humans ought to be the master of this planet, not animals. Some may say, how can we determine among over seven billion beings, which are the humans and which are the animals! It's simpler than it sounds. A creature that values human life above everything else, is a human, all others are animals - and I mean above everything else - above tradition, above heritage, above culture, above religion, above politics, above partisanism, above intellect, above reason, above freedom, above opinion above habit and above what one is used to or not used to.

Let me be a bit more articulate with a few examples. A scientist who shouts at a layperson, *"I don't care what you believe"* - is an animal. A preacher who shouts at a person of different faith, *"you are going to hell, until you accept my God as one true God"* - is an animal. A civilian who denies to stay home during a pandemic, shouting *"sacrifice the weak and live free"* - is an animal. A president who says *"white skin is racially superior"* - is an animal.

In short, a creature that places more importance on other things than human life, is not worth the title human. The bigots may say to me, in fact, they have shouted at me on several occasions, *"how dare you insult us people"* - to them I say, I do not insult people, for if they were people in the first place, they wouldn't insult humankind by looking down on human life. They may call me mad for this, so let me put it even straighter.

Yes I am mad, I am insane - everybody is mad for something, I am mad for my humankind. I am mad – I am drunk with the elixir of harmony and unification. I have drunk the elixir of revolution, what good is alcohol for me! There is no greater intoxication than the intoxication of revolution - there is no higher high than being high on revolution - and this very high is what delivers humanity liberation, but not just any liberation, civilized liberation (we'll investigate the difference later on). Without this high there would be no civilized world to speak of.

Where there is no revolution, there is no progress, where there is no progress, there is no difference between human life and animal life. So, if we want to stand apart from the animals, if we want to stand out amidst the 8.7 million species of planet earth - we must possess an indomitable desire for collective upliftment. And you can't lift a society by following the crowd that's going downhill with discrimination and prejudice - you must stand out, alone and unbending, as the epitome of life, liberty and collective prosperity.

5. Standing Alone, Not Separate

Now the question that rises is, if you stand out as the lone pillar of upliftment, separate from the intentions of the crowd, how can you represent the collective! Here what we must first realize is that, standing out as a beacon of humanity instead of following the crowd, doesn't mean standing separate from the society, instead it means standing as an unified example of an entire human society - it means the individual representing the collective, but not the way the collective behaves, but the way a human collective ought to behave.

One of the fundamental facts of social psyche is that without the living embodiments of humanity, the society would never ever feel the urge to act humane, despite having the capacity of humaneness within. So, in short, heroes don't stand in line, they set out alone into the unknown and lines form behind them. And if a handful of heroes didn't set out alone to explore the unknown, we'd still be living in the jungle.

So, it's imperative that no matter the course that others take, you the individual being of conscience and character do what's right, and not what's easy or usual. The term usual is only relevant for a lifeform in complacency, and a lifeform that has gone complacent, freezes in the face of catastrophe and eventually perishes, whereas a lifeform which is never too afraid to tread into unknown territory, is more likely to survive a catastrophe.

But here we must understand one thing - an entire species can never collectively tread into unknown territory, unless a handful of members of that species take the first step - these are the leaders - the pioneers - the pathfinders of progress. And they are present in every time and age, for if they don't, then humankind would come to a standstill. Without the torchbearers, all we'll have left is darkness. Now comes the most important - what are you? Never forget, wherever there is darkness, there is need for light. In fact, in every darkness there is possibility of light.

And even in this day and age, our so-called modern human society is filled with dark corners. Take religion for example. Even today, despite being an intricately interconnected global species, a substantial portion of the human population is incapable of truly practicing the realization of religious harmony in their life. They still use the term "god-fearing" to define themselves, as a way of showing their loyalty to their so-called faith. They talk most boastfully about the lord being merciful, yet their behavior only exudes hate, prejudice, terror and an absolute ignorance of practical holiness.

Those who obey without contemplation, never attains holiness. They only waste their potential in living a delusion. If you wish to worship the lord, do so with love, not terror - if you desire to practice faith, let that faith be guided by tenderness, not bitterness - if you want others to understand your outlook, use friendliness, not force. Remember this golden principle of religion - a religion with compulsion is no religion. A religion that teaches segregation instead of inclusion, is no religion. A religion that preaches violence as a method to counter criticism and disagreement, is anything but religion.

Hence, it's up to each one of the conscientious beings of this planet to redefine the very paradigm of religion – we must do away with the very term "organized" from the domain of religion.

Forget organized religions - forget scriptures - forget gods, fathers, sons and spirits - forget all dogmas taught by the representatives of theoretical religion, and then only you shall be able to visualize the true core of religion. Religion is in you my friend. It rises from the human mind for the good of the human society. Its God is the human self, and the worshiper is the human self. Religion is the self revealing secrets of the self to the self.

In the world of primitive savages, religion and bigotry go hand in hand. But, in the world of civilized humans, religion and reason must go hand in hand. Religion without reason is merely an illusion of religion – it is a mockery of religion, like it has become today. Religion without reason is like making love without love. Remember my friend, religion lies not where reign bigotry, prejudice and hate. It is only through reason and a concern for all, one will discover true religion.

Each one of us must do our part to counter the attacks of hatred with slogans of love. We must become the slogan of love ourselves, for once we do, all separation disappears. Christ and I are one - Jehovah and I are one - Buddha and I are one - Nanak and I are one - Mohammed and I are one - you and I are one - separation exists where there is no love, but where reigns love, separation fades away.

6. Love Beyond Philosophies

Many people often use the term philosophy of love, but here's the fact of the matter - there is no such thing as a philosophy of love. Calling love a philosophy is like calling the air we breathe a philosophy or the water we drink a philosophy or the ground we stand on a philosophy. Love is the very foundation of human existence. Without love, it's not a human existence to begin with. We could find tons of things that we could philosophize but love is not one of them. A human is either love incarnate, or not human at all. Every other human is merely a mockery of humanhood.

A true human celebrates being annihilated for others - a true human guards their community, their neighborhood, their society, from the invasion of inhumanity - a true human never thinks twice before lending a hand to those in distress - a true human finds meaning in life by adding colors to the lives of others.

Remember, fire is power. Before there was life, there was fire. That fire is still inside all of us, which can never be extinguished. Any discrimination that comes close, will burn to ashes - any prejudice that comes close, will turn to dust - any injustice that comes close, will get extinct. You are the fire incarnate - keep burning - keep burning - keep burning for the people - keep burning for the community - keep burning for the society - keep burning for humanity.

Justice starts with you. Liberty starts with you. Progress starts with you. To put it simply, the world starts with you. Character of the individual becomes the character of the world. When the individual is conflicted, the world is conflicted - when the individual is at peace, the world is at peace. It all starts with you. Humans are both the disease and the cure in the societal physiology. This means that for every societal disease there is a cure lurking around in one human or another. Now the question is, why can't that cure be you! Be the cure that you seek elsewhere.

7. Medicine for Society

Every human is a potential medicine for the society. You know what medicine means! MEDICINE means Mercy - Empathy - Dare - Integrity - Care - Ingenuity – Nobility and Ethics. From the outside these qualities may look different, but in practice they are all one force for good. Let's investigate how.

What is a human without mercy - not a human. What is a human without empathy - not a human. Likewise, all these qualities define the very existence of a true human being - they distinguish human life from animal life. Hence, any human who is a true human, automatically turns into a medicine for the society. And based on the paths chosen by these humans, they are hailed differently. Some are called scientists - some are called teachers - some are called doctors - some are called cops - and so on.

Those who treat the darkness of the unknown, are called scientists - those who treat the ignorance in the budding minds, are called teachers - those who treat the darkness of ailments in individuals, are called doctors - those who treat the darkness of chaos in the society, are called cops - and so on. Each human being on this planet is a potential medicine, for each human being holds in their nerves the capacity to heal the wounds and sicknesses of our society.

Being a gateway to wellness for others is far more important than being a walking encyclopedia. And as I have said previously, wellness is not the lack of sickness, wellness is the capacity to overcome sickness. For example, symptoms of a sickness are not necessarily signs of weakness, rather they imply that your body is actively fighting the sickness. Likewise, a revolution is not a sign of a sick society, it's the sign of a healthy society trying to fight oppression and inhumanity.

Shred all selfishness and become the capacity of wellness for the society - hold the torch of wellness and liberty high with your spine upright, so that every sickness trembles at the very sight of you. Remember, law is a myth, it's not going to ensure order and justice in the world - order and justice can only prevail when the humans actually realize in their bones the repercussions of their own actions in the society.

And when I say, in the society, I am not separating public life and private life - this very separation is a sign of a hypocritical society. Public and private are not separate - that is, they cannot be separate in a civilized society. If you are one person in your private life and completely another in public, then you are essentially building a fake society - a society that stands on the grounds of lies - and a society that is erected on the grounds of lies is destined to fall. No society can last long on the grounds of lies, on the grounds of superficiality. Only on the grounds of truthfulness, can we raise a healthy, humane, responsible and progressive society.

How can you expect the society to be truthful when you yourself pretend to be a different person than you actually are! And how can you possibly expect for such society to understand the value of integrity, honesty and character! Remember, integrity of the society is predicated on the integrity of the individual - it's predicated on your integrity. Whatever happens to our society is the responsibility of nobody else' but yours - it's the responsibility of each one of us.

8. Family and Society Are One

A huge portion of the population lives under the delusion that the problems of the society are the responsibility of the politicians and civil servants. For example, a person came up to me at an airport a while back and said most earnestly, *"you are a scientist, why do you bother with social issues."* I paused for a while gasping at his sheer callousness and replied - I am not just a scientist, I am a human - when a beast invades your house and starts abusing your loved ones, would you sit back waiting for the authorities to intervene - you may, but I can't - I won't - for me family and society are one, and when wild animals run rampant abusing that family of mine, I would die defending my family, not sit back like a spineless coward. My science is not separate from my humanity - they fulfill each other - they empower each other.

Every human is my people, and if some savage so much as touches even a hair on their head, I'll chop off every single head of such inhumanity (not to be taken literally, although it can be literal under dire circumstances, for which even the law has provision, but there are countless ways to incapacitate a person without actually committing homicide).

Time and again the need arises for one fierce sword of character to stand face to face with the inhumans and bigots, and announce with an earth-shaking fervor - from this moment on, you are only inches away from extinction - at night look closely to every shadow - and by the light of day know that I am just one step behind you - mark me - one sinister move, one malicious deed and I will swoop down on you like god's thunder - from this moment on, I own your evil heart, and I will crush it, if you hurt the people anymore.

9. Nature's Gift to Us

Revolution for justice is not violence, it's conscience. Standing up to savagery is not violence, it's human sentience. Sentience as advanced as ours is there so that we could stand up to nonsense. However, if we choose to submit to nonsense instead, then our sentience is no more advanced than the animals. To be more than animals, we must act more than animals.

What makes us biologically superior to the animals is our extensive line of brain capacities, which all other animals lack - most of their brain capacity goes to powering the basic functionings of their body, and whatever capacity is left goes to the basic cognitive tasks required to survive in the jungle - after carrying out all these tasks, there is no power left in their brain for extra-survival activity. But when it comes to us humans, our ancestors crossed the boundaries of survival-need long time ago with sheer ingenuity and boldness - and having done so, they had both time and brain capacity to engage in other activities, such as science, philosophy, arts, sports and so on.

For example, once they learnt to control and create fire, it not only gave them a substantial upper hand against wild animals and darkness, but it also enabled them to cook their meals, and the nutrition from cooked meat added more neural capacity to their brain. Then each new innovation made way for further extra-survival activities, both cognitive and behavioral.

Eventually, our species broke all ties with the wild and built a completely new kingdom for themselves, separate from the life-threatening toils of the wilderness. However, this new kingdom, which we call civilization, is not exactly separate from Nature, rather it's merely separate from rest of the animal kingdom. While the animals remain completely at the mercy of Nature, we on the other hand, though still rely on Nature to provide us with food, air and water, our reliance on Nature is far too little in comparison to other animals.

We have learnt to tame the forces of Nature and use them at our disposal however we see fit. And our attempt to tame Nature has made our brain circuits more complex, which in turn has made us more capable of taming Nature. Our prolonged struggles in the wild accompanied by certain uniquely human choices and feats have made our brain develop capacities previously undeveloped in any other species on earth.

The capacities that we are born with are Nature's gift to us and how we use them is our gift to Nature. We have developed capacities so grand that we have actually started to comprehend the possibility of stepping outside planet earth and colonizing another planet. Can you imagine the gravitas of such daring dream! And I am more convinced now than ever that this dream will become reality, perhaps within the next thousand years. However, to those involved in space exploration, I have one thing to say - we cannot become a successful race of space explorers with traditional rocket and jet propulsion drive - we need to come up with a cooler and lasting alternative.

Now to get back to the matter at hand - space exploration is only one of many of the astounding feats we have accomplished. Think of weather prediction for example. With the rise of artificial intelligence based weather prediction models as well as data gathered through space explorations, we are now able to issue storm warning much earlier so that people could take precautions, which would have been impossible a few centuries ago. Or think of the advancements we have made in medical science, which has increased average life-span exponentially.

However the irony of the matter is that, we are better at taming the forces of nature outside of us, than the forces of nature inside of us. Furthermore, children are taught from a very early age to look outside, but never to look inside - they are given lessons on math, physics, chemistry, biology and on countless more subjects, but not the lessons on character.

Lessons of character can be given to the kids only by being a being of character yourself, the lack of which has filled this society with egotistical and insecure snobs. The parents cannot be sure of their children's safety even while leaving them alone with a teacher, because, even the term teacher doesn't say anything about a person's character.

Quite the same way - the term scientist says nothing about a person's character - the term preacher says nothing about a person's character - the term believer says nothing about a person's character - the term atheist says nothing about a person's character - the term freethinker says nothing about a person's character - and terms like rational, spiritual, humanist, democratic, republican, capitalist, socialist and idealist say nothing about a person's character.

In short, neither intelligence nor religion is the sign of a good human being. And a human without goodness is no human, no matter how intelligent they are or how strong their faith in almighty is. Goodness requires a humble heart, but unfortunately the clouds of intelligence as well as religion often cast a shadow on that humility and turn a human into a bigoted and arrogant savage.

Intellect that takes away your humility isn't worth a penny. I would rather lose my intellect than my humility. And perhaps I already did, for my works are not work of the so-called intellect - may be a few of my earliest works were the work of intellect, but not the later once since "In Search of Divinity". I simply walk the meadows of truth while occasionally picking up one or two flowers to share with the world - but one life is too short to walk the entirety of the meadows. In fact, the meadows of truth are spread across infinity for the curious and humble to remain awestruck forever.

10. The Phantom of Truth

Truth is beyond the knowable and unknowable. Truth is endless and timeless, yet never is it closer to you than the times when you are naively curious. Truth reveals itself to the inquisitive and runs away from the bigots and cynics. If you are curious - and I mean, naively curious, that is, without any expectation to reach a certain destination or conclusion, then truth is yours to command, but if you are a stickler for tradition or busting with pride about your intellect, then you can chase the illusive phantom of truth your whole life and not find an ounce of it.

Pride and arrogance are enemies of truth, for they are the enemies of everything that's gentle in nature - they are the enemies of nature. Truth is nature and to understand nature you must be humble as ashes and vigorous as the wind. Nature doesn't reveal her secrets to the arrogant, for nature is at nobody's mercy - she only reveals her secrets to the humble.

And as I have said before, it's only the humble learner of today who becomes a strong leader of tomorrow. Humility makes the mind fertile and a fertile mind is a breeding ground for excellence, and excellence breeds achievement.

To put it simply, truth is no big deal, if you can step firmly on the grounds of reason while fostering acceptance for the weakness of others. Knowledge alone is futile, unless it's guided by the intention of benefitting all.

Only by standing together and not against each other, will any of us stand at all. And when people are too afraid or insecure to stand up, become their courage yourself and take away their insecurity by standing alone against all odds and soon they'll muster the courage and inspiration to stand next to you. You cannot simply tell them to stand up, you can only be a living epitome of righteousness and bravery in front of their eyes, and their own conscience will do the rest.

11. More Than Money, Give Me Society

Humans are a magnificent species, not because of intelligence mark you, intelligence has very little to do with it. Humans are magnificent because they have the capacity to empathize even to the absurd point of self-annihilation, if they are given the right push, either by circumstances or by an individual with an indomitable commitment to society.

More than money, fame and romance, I crave for society - such should be the fervor of an individual who wants to wake up the world from the sleep of indifference. Mind not the mockery, mind not the agony, mind not even death, and destroy yourself for the people and the people will change. Change of a people starts with an individual.

Where there is no individual, there is no society. But individual doesn't mean separate, it means indivisible. However, the popular belief on the term individual is that it means being different, and as a result, most of the human population have no comprehension whatsoever of either the content or nature of "individuality".

Individuality means not being different, it means not losing one's identity in a mindless attempt to be accepted by the crowd. Individuality means retaining one's identity, not through the practice of egotism, but with an indomitable sense of dignity. When you do not pretend to be someone you are not, you have nothing to worry about, because those who cannot accept you as you are with all your imperfections, have no bearing over your life whatsoever. Here, I am not advocating for arrogance or pride, as you would've realized by now, instead I am referring to a plain, ordinary stubbornness to not lose your integrity in the cacophony of snobbery and bootlicking.

This is also the reason, I feel, think and behave the same, whether I am talking to a president of a nation, a scholar, a janitor or a sex worker. I have nothing to hide and nothing to gain, hence I have no need for pretense. I am who I am, all the time everywhere. In fact, many admirers often come to me at various events and ask me that, I should not be so simple to everybody, instead I should appear more serious - and my reply to such concern is always the same - my work as an expert of human behavior only makes me a servant of humankind, it definitely doesn't place me aloof from the everyday joys and sorrows of human life, then why on earth should I pretend to be anything but a simple human being. I am not a machine and I have no desire to be one.

Remember, while the serious rushes to reach the destination with no concern for the sweetness of life, the simple and the humble relishes every moment of the journey with no concern whatsoever for ever reaching the destination. As far as the simple mind is concerned, it's already living the destination by losing the self in the journey.

Lose yourself in the journey and before you know it, you would've already reached the destination and started a new journey towards a new destination. So long as we live, destinations will never end, hence the destination won't give you joy, what will is the journey, once you let go of your desire to reach somewhere. Just live, feel, think and act - leave the rest to nature, that's the best way to bring about change in one's life as well as one's society.

Society can't be changed with seriousness or cynicism, it can only be changed with simplicity and love. And a society that's changed with seriousness and cynicism becomes harsh and tasteless over time. Is that the kind of society you want for your children - for our children! Remember, simplicity is the sign of a loving and alive mind, whereas cynicism is the sign of a dull and mechanical mind.

Love is like the cool breeze that comes through the window after a night of heavy rain and gently caresses your cheeks like the palm of a caring mother and when it does, you don't sit down to analyze the velocity of the wind, you just close your eyes and become vulnerable to every whiff of it and let it be absorbed by every follicle on your skin. The more you analyze love, the more you lose its meaning. So, don't analyze, don't criticize, don't philosophize, don't intellectualize, just let it be - and let yourself be.

Be brave enough to be lost and you'll discover a land most magnificent. Insecurity breeds nothing good, but bravery does - bravery breeds change - bravery breeds progress - bravery breeds everything that's worth having in life.

Be not scared to sail into the storm, every storm reveals the jewels of life. Be not scared to walk into the dark, your footsteps are the very light the dark is afraid of. There is no dark that can be the doom to humanity, so long as you stand as the doom to that very dark. Be the light unto the dark and even the thought of casting an evil gaze on humanity would perish from the foul hearts.

12. Progress Favors The Brave

Foul hearts make foul society, and the only way to prevent that is to be the antidote to that foulness ourselves. Stand up to every foul act with an unbending dignity and unbound conscience. Boil your character well over the flames of conscience - as long as there are impurities, there'll be a stinking smoke, but once the impurities are burnt out (in case of human psyche, they won't go away, but they can turn ineffective), there is neither smoke nor smell - all that remains is a pure, luminous, ever-effulgent character - a character that can't be bound by no labels nor dogmas.

Such is the character that's needed to guard the society against the darkness that lurks in the animal corners of the human heart. What is animal, what is human, can't be determined by appearance, it's only determined by action. Be conscious of your actions - let your actions be driven by your conscience - let your conscience be driven by responsibility - let your responsibility be driven by your humanity.

In an almost maniacal pursuit of productivity, humankind has lost sight of its humanity. Do not let that happen my friend! I repeat, do not let humankind lose its humanity. How can you, one person, stop that from happening you ask - stand up yourself amidst the society as a daring reminder to humanity.

It's this simple, either you change the society, or the society changes you - and the only way to change the society is to never lose faith in yourself, even if the whole world turns against you. Change favors the brave - progress favors the brave. Because all change, all progress begins with the brave, not the spineless coward.

Some may say, they are not coward, they are just cautious. To them I say, cowardly and cautious are two different things. Cautious means that you have taken into consideration every possible danger, whereas coward means, you've gotten too used to inaction. Cautiousness can sometimes lead you to not act, but when that happens, it's only because in such circumstances, action would cause more harm than inaction. And though this may sound a bit preposterous to some, but here what we must keep in mind is that nothing in this world is black and white - our entire societal fabric is filled with grey areas.

So, be observant of the situation and take action accordingly. Be headstrong but make sure that that that head has wisdom in it too. A headstrong individual without wisdom is like a running vehicle without a driver. Such a vehicle can achieve great distances and discover terrific new destinations, but only if wisdom is behind the wheel.

13. There's A Candle in You

Every thinker is tempted to say that their work possesses all the answer in the world. But such is only an intellectual stupidity. Hence, I can never say, I have all the answers to your problems. The answer to the problems of your life is you - they hide deep inside your mind. But, you need to have novelty in thought for those answers to come to the surface. Probe your mind with an intense zeal and an indomitable will, and it'll reveal to you the answers to even the most difficult problems.

The human mind has a candle inside. For most humans that candle only flickers through life. But for the observant that candle burns so bright that it engulfs every corner of the land it steps foot on. A few candles in every corner of the world can light up the entire planet. But the trouble with humankind is that they sit idle in their cocoon of insecurity, hoping for someone else to burn their candle while forgetting about the 60 watt (that's about how much energy the human brain runs on) powerhouse they each possess in front of which all the power stations in the world turn powerless.

The power is yours - and it lives inside your skull. The human brain is the single most magnificent organic structure that nature has ever devised. And you won't realize the gravitas of the matter until you go deeper. Every single human achievement that we see in this world has its origin in the brain - in the electrochemical impulses amidst the neurons.

From the wheel to the steel - from papyrus to kindle - from churchbell to doorbell - from holy books to comic books - from monotheism to secularism - from fundamentalism to humanism - from steam engine to jet engine - from cave painting to apple pencil - from antibiotics to antipsychotics - from embroidery to surgery - from moving pics to netflix - every single feat that we can think of, good or bad, is born of the neurons. In short, neurons can make the world or break the world.

14. No Revolution, No Destiny

Human civilization is born of neurons. But here we must keep in mind that though we are using the term civilization due to all the extraordinary feats accomplished by humankind, we are yet to be truly civilized in our psyche. As I said earlier, there is an animal lurking in the dark corners of the human mind. Only when you become aware of that animal and bring it under your conscious control, can true civilization manifest in your mind - and when civilization manifests inside the mind it automatically is reflected into the world outside.

So, first be aware, then take action - that's the golden principle behind every revolution - be it a revolution in mind or a revolution in society. In fact, the very distinction between mental and societal revolution is a phantom, for revolution in society starts with revolution in mind.

One woman had the revolution in mind that she had the right to a seat in a bus just like any other person - that led to a man having the revolution in mind that one day our land of liberty would no longer discriminate people on the basis of color, and that revolution in turn led to the revolution in society, which we today celebrate as the civil rights movement. Now this is only one example. History of humankind is replete with such countless instances that moulded the very destiny of our species.

In fact, revolution breeds destiny - no revolution no destiny - make this motto your life and upliftment will follow your trail on its own. Destiny is an illusion - it is one of those ideas that were born of ignorance, not knowledge. What is the reason behind such invention some may wonder! And the answer is quite simple. It is common tendency of the human mind to fill in the gaps in understanding with imagination. And besides destiny, this tendency has caused the birth of humankind's most treasured beliefs - such as reincarnation, deities, ghosts, trinity, astrology, afterlife and so on.

The basic evolutionary reason behind the birth of these notions is simple, it's not to foster understanding but to eliminate insecurity over the unknown. And that is also the reason why these beliefs have survived amidst the rise of reason and curiosity. However, these beliefs are not necessarily the problem, the problem is when a person holds on to their beliefs even at the cost of harming others.

An existential fact about the human mind is that it cannot function without beliefs, however, in order to make sure that our beliefs do not do harm to others as well as ourselves, we must at all times be in full control of our beliefs and if at any moment we find a certain belief to do more harm than good, then we must muster the courage to throw away such belief, even if it means going against centuries old traditions.

15. O My Dear Earthling (A Sonnet)

O My Dear Earthling (A Sonnet)

O My Dear Earthling open your doors,
For the supreme festival has arrived.
The whole wide nature is rejoicing in love,
Step outside cultures and celebrate life.
The sky is engulfed with billions of smiles,
Smiles that know not pettiness of society.
Open your soul O Mighty Earthling,
The wind of amity is here bearing unity.
No more bounds on love, race and religion,
Prejudice suits not a species of sapiens.
Value we must character over conformity,
It's time we throw away all our allegiance.
On guard we stand against differentiation,
Hear all peddlers of hate – we are all one.

16. Drumbeats of Conscience

Traditions are never more important than humans - beliefs are never more important than humans. The fabric of society should be crafted according to the measures of conscience and character, not dogmas, traditions, beliefs, greed, superficiality and egotism. In fact, the time has come for the grand revolution against millennia old tradition of indifference to manifest.

As I have said in Operation Justice, "injustice won't destroy the world, indifference will." So, open your eyes and break out like a pandemic from the age-old sleep of indifference and rush to the length and breadth of your society as a living torch of humaneness. Mind not if nobody else wakes up, wake yourself up and your titanic steps will resound through each corner of the society as the drumbeats of conscience. Each step of yours is a blessing to all, just take the first step and see.

Why would you bother to follow the crowd - what are you afraid of - do away with the fear my friend - grow bigger than your fears and your feet will do wonders. Nature has given you legs, not to travel the safe and common road, but to discover new territory - to draw new maps. Nature has given you a mind, not to think comfortable thoughts, but to embark into the most daring expedition - expedition in thought - expedition in perception - expedition in sentience - expedition in fervor. Only from such original expedition can a revolution be born. Revolution doesn't follow the crowd, the crowd follows the revolution.

Don't start a revolution, be the revolution. And to be the revolution, it is imperative that you break your obedience to the crowd. Remember, yesmen only enjoy progress and pass comments, but they don't cause progress. So, be bold and conscientious enough to distinguish the right from the wrong, even if the wrong is accepted as right by thousands or even millions. The truth doesn't turn less true, because it has no followers.

However, here I must mention one thing, those who use the term truth to refer to the supernatural and paranormal, are no more seekers of truth than the infant who takes pleasure in fairytales. Nevertheless, whether it's a child that believes in fairytales or an adult, in both cases it's a matter of self-preservation, it has nothing to do with truth. Those who understand this, for them fairytales can be healthy, as much as any other kind of fictitious story, but in the hands of those who confuse fairytales with facts, they can cause great harm to societal health and harmony.

17. Observation without Allegiance

Be bold enough to observe yourself - your thoughts - your feelings, your beliefs - observe them like you'd observe them in another person - and I say observe, not analyze or criticize. Revolution can bring forth the most progressive outcome, especially through those who are self-observant. When you observe yourself better, you observe the society better.

And this observation has no allegiance to any authority - it has no label attached to it - you don't observe as a communist or capitalist - you don't observe as a feminist or humanist - you don't observe as a believer or non-believer - you don't observer as a liberal or conservative - you just observe with your whole being without the bounds of labels. That's the only kind of practical observation there is, every other observation is merely conformity in disguise.

Certain labels may have served their purpose in the past, but in a global and inclusive society they only impede progress and disrupt harmony. Let me give you an example. Choosing between capitalism and socialism to run the world is like choosing between man and woman to run the world. These choices may have been relevant in the old days, but in a civilized world they are absolutely meaningless.

To ensure rights and equality for everyone, we must free ourselves from the age-old loyalty to labels and ideologies. Otherwise, we'll only keep on repeating the mistakes of our ancestors and replace one form of injustice with another. Remember, replacing one tyrannical paradigm with another is not progress, it's only recurring regress. So, if you think your paradigm is better than the one that exists, think again.

In most circumstances, people use the term revolution as a means to liberation from an oppressive regime, while merely trying to replace the old regime with a new one. But here is the point, the purpose of revolution is not liberation, it's self-determination. To some they may appear to be the same. But they are not, for self-determination entails accountability, whereas liberation does not. Liberation is far too puny a term in front of the grand responsibility that comes along with self-determination. Without this fundamental sense of responsibility, revolution only makes way for new oppressors.

18. Hurricane Humans (A Sonnet)

Hurricane Humans (A Sonnet)

Come all ye misfits and rebels,
Let's march to shatter the games.
Break all golden chains of comfort,
Let's work forgetting our names.
Come all ye sneered and mocked,
We must burn as flames of unity.
Let's turn into a human tsunami,
And wash away all hate and rigidity.
Hurricane humans we are o brethren,
Savagery no more is master to us.
The fountain of inclusion is our lifeblood,
We won't let tradition break our universe.
Let's finally build the kingdom of heaven,
With clay from our heart's unifying Eden.

19. Becoming Revolution Incarnate

Liberation alone doesn't solve anything, people must have the understanding of how to live that liberation in a civilized manner, or else human liberation and animal liberation would turn the same. In the animal world one animal's liberation is not concerned with the wellbeing of other animals, whereas in the human world this can't be the case. A human ought to be concerned for the wellbeing of others, as though they are one's own reflection, which they are.

All humans are innately one, this is the driving force behind all revolution. All that we call ethics and morality is but a manifestation of this oneness. All that we call love is a manifestation of this oneness. Without this oneness, there is no revolution. Without this oneness, there is no progress. Without this oneness, there is no civilization.

The moment you realize, by hurting someone you hurt yourself and by loving someone you love yourself, you become an exuberant embodiment of revolution absolute. When a person has reached the highest, when they see neither man nor woman, neither black nor white, neither belief nor disbelief, nor any other sects and differentiation, but looks at a person beyond the brandings, then alone has the person attained universal oneness - and such a person is the true revolution incarnate – such a person is the very lifeblood of revolution indomitable.

BIBLIOGRAPHY

Aristotle. Politics. Penguin; Revised, Reprint edition. (2000)

Aristotle. De Anima (On the Soul). Penguin Random House. 1987

Aristotle. Physics. Kessinger Publishing, 2004

Archer M., (2000), Being Human: The Problem of Agency. Cambridge University Press.

Archer M., (2003), Structure, Agency and the Internal Conversation. Cambridge University Press.

Adolphs R (2003) Cognitive neuroscience of human social behaviour. Nature Rev Neurosci 4: 165–178.

Adolphs R, Tranel D, Damasio AR (2003) Dissociable neural systems for recognizing emotions. Brain Cogn 52: 61–69.

Afton, A. D. (1985). Forced copulation as a reproductive strategy of male lesser scaup: A field test of some predictions. - Behaviour 92, p. 146-167.

Allison T, Puce A, McCarthy G. (2000) Social perception from visual cues: role of the STS region. Trends Cogn Sci 4: 267–278.

Andresen, Jensine, and Robert Forman, eds. Cognitive Models and Spiritual Maps. Bowling Green, Ohio: Imprint Academic, 2000.

Ashbrook, James, and Carol Albright. The Humanizing Brain: Where Religion and Neuroscience Meet. Cleveland, OH: Pilgrim Press, 1997.

Azari, Nina, Janpeter Nickel, Gilbert Wunderlich, Michael Niedeggen, Harald Hefter, Lutz Tellmann, Hans Herzog, Petra Stoerig, Dieter Birnbacher, and Rudiger Seitz. "Neural Correlates of Religious Experience."

European Journal of Neuroscience 13, no. 8 (2001)

Agar, N. (2004). Liberal eugenics: In defence of human enhancement. London: Blackwell Publishing.

Alteheld, N., Roessler, G., Vobig, M., & Walter, R. (2004). The retina implant new approach to a visual prosthesis. Biomedizinische Technik, 49(4), 99–103.

Antal, A., Nitsche, M. A., Kincses, T. Z., Kruse, W., Hoffmann, K. P., & Paulus, W. (2004a). Facilitation of visuo-motor learning by transcranial direct current stimulation of the motor and extrastriate visual areas in humans. European Journal of Neuroscience, 19(10), 2888–2892.

Bhat Z, Kumar, S, Bhat H (2015) In vitro meat production. Challenges and benefits over conventional meat production. J Sci Food Agric 14: 241–248

Bernstein R. J., (1967), John Dewey. New York: Washington Square Press.

Bernstein R.J., (1971), Praxis and Action: Contemporary Philosophies of Human Activity. Philadelphia: University of Pennsylvania Press.

Bernstein R.J., (1976), The Restructuring Social and Political Thought.

Bernstein R.J., (1983), Beyond Relativism and Objectivism: Science, Hermeneutics, and Praxis. Philadelphia: University of Pennsylvania Press.

Bernstein R.J., (1986), Philosophical Profiles. Philadelphia: University of Pennsylvania Press.

Bernstein R.J., (1991), New Constellation. Cambridge: MIT Press.

Barash, D. P. (1977). Sociobiology of rape in mallards (Anas platyrhynchos):

Responses of the mated male. - Science 197, p. 788-789.

Berger, J. (1986). Wild horses of the great basin: Social competition and population size. - The University of Chicago Press, Chicago.

Birkhead, T. R., Johnson, S. D. & Nettleship, D. N. (1985). Extra-pair matings and mate guarding in the common murre Uria aalge. - Anim. Behav. 33, p. 608-619.

Beauregard, Mario, and Vincent Paquette. "Neural Correlates of a Mystical Experience in Carmelite Nuns." Neuroscience Letters 405, no. 3 (2006)

Benson, Herbert. Timeless Healing: The Power and Biology of Belief. New York: Scribner, 1996

Bogen, J.E.(1995a), 'On the neurophysiology of consciousness: Part I. An overview', Consciousness and Cognition, 4.

Bogen, J.E. (1995b), 'On the neurophysiology of consciousness: Part II. Constraining the semantic problem', Consciousness and Cognition, 4.

Bremner, J. D., R. Soufer, et al. (2001). "Gender differences in cognitive and neural correlates of remembrance of emotional words." Psychopharmacol Bull 35 (3).

Brothers, L. (2002). The social brain: A project for integrating primate behavior and neurophysiology in a new domain. In J. T. Cacioppo et al. (Eds.), Foundations in neuroscience. Cambridge, MA: MIT Press.

Buss, D. D. (2003). Evolutionary Psychology: The New Science of Mind, 2nd ed. New York: Allyn & Bacon.

Buss, D. M. (1989). "Conflict between the sexes: Strategic interference and the evocation of anger and upset." J Pers Soc Psychol 56 (5).

Buss, D. M. (1995). "Psychological sex differences. Origins through sexual selection." Am Psychol 50 (3).

Buss, D. M. (2002). "Review: Human Mate Guarding." Neuro Endocrinol Lett 23 (Suppl 4).

Buss, D. M., and D. P. Schmitt (1993). "Sexual strategies theory: An evolutionary perspective on human mating." Psychol Rev 100 (2).

Blakemore SJ, Decety J (2001) From the perception of action to the understanding of intention. Nature Rev Neurosci 2: 561.

Bruce C, Desimone R, Gross CG (1981) Visual properties of neurons in a polysensory area in superior temporal sulcus of the macaque. J Neurophysiol 46: 369–384.

Buccino G, Vogt S, Ritzl A, Fink GR, Zilles K, Freund HJ, Rizzolatti G (2004) Neural circuits underlying imitation of hand actions: an event related fMRI study. Neuron 42: 323–34.

Colapietro V., (1988), "Human Agency: The Habits of Our Being." Southern Journal of Philosophy, XXVI, 2, pp. 153-68.

Colapietro V., (1992), "Purpose, Power, and Agency." The Monist, 75, 4 (October) pp. 423-44.

Colapietro V., (2003), "Signs and their vicissitudes: Meanings in excess of consciousness and functionality." Logica, Dialogica, Ideologica, a cure di Susan Petrilli e Patrizia Calefato (Milano: Mimesis), pp. 221-36.

Colapietro V., (2004a), "C. S. Peirce's Reclamation of Teleology." Nature in American Philosophy, ed. Jean De Groot (Washington, D.C.: Catholic University Press of America), pp. 88-108.

Colapietro V., (2004b), "Portrait of a Historicist: An Alternative Reading of

Peircean Semiotic." Semiotiche, 2/04 [maggio 2004], pp. 49-68.

Colapietro V., (2006), "Engaged Pluralism: Between Alterity and Sociality." The Pragmatic Century: Conversations with Richard J. Bernstein (Albany, NY: SUNY Press), pp. 39-68.

Colapietro V., (2009), "Habit, Competence, and Purpose." Forthcoming in The Transactions of the Charles S. Peirce Society. Calder AJ, Keane J, Manes F, Antoun N, Young AW (2000) Impaired recognition and experience of disgust following brain injury. Nature Neurosci 3: 1077–1078.

Carey DP, Perrett DI, Oram MW (1997) Recognizing, understanding and reproducing actions. In: Jeannerod M, Grafman J (eds) Handbook of neuropsychology. Vol. 11: Action and cognition. Elsevier, Amsterdam.

Carr L, Iacoboni M, Dubeau MC, Mazziotta JC, Lenzi GL (2003) Neural mechanisms of empathy in humans: a relay from neural systems for imitation to limbic areas. Proc Natl Acad Sci USA 100: 5497–5502.

Changeux JP, Ricoeur P (1998) La nature et la règle. Odile Jacob, Paris.

Cochin S, Barthelemy C, Roux S, Martineau J (1999) Observation and execution of movement: similarities demonstrated by quantified electroencephalograpy. Eur J Neurosci 11: 1839– 1842.

Chomsky Noam, (2017) Requiem for the American Dream

Chomsky Noam, (2016) Who Rules the World?

Chomsky Noam, (2010) How the World Works

Churchland, P.S. (1986), Neurophilosophy (Cambridge, MA: The MIT Press).

Churchland, P.S. & Ramachandran, V.S. (1993), 'Filling in: Why Dennett is wrong', in Dennett and His Critics: Demystifying Mind, ed. B. Dahlbom (Oxford: Blackwell Scientific Press).

Churchland, P.S., Ramachandran, V.S. & Sejnowski, T.J. (1994), 'A critique of pure vision', in Large- scale Neuronal Theories of the Brain, ed. C. Koch & J.L. Davis (Cambridge, MA: The MIT Press).

Crick, F. (1994), The Astonishing Hypothesis: The Scientific Search for the Soul (New York: Simon and Schuster).

Crick, F. (1996), 'Visual perception: rivalry and consciousness', Nature, 379.

Crick, F. & Koch, C. (1992), 'The problem of consciousness', Scientific American, 267.

Craig AD (2002) How do you feel? Interoception: the sense of the physiological condition of the body. Nature Rev Neurosci 3: 655–666.

Damasio, A (2003a) Looking for Spinoza. Harcourt Inc. Damasio A (2003b) Feeling of emotion and the self. Ann NY Acad Sci 1001: 253–261.

d'Aquili, Eugene. "Senses of Reality in Science and Religion." Zygon 17, no 4 (1982)

d'Aquili, Eugene. "The Biopsychological Determinants of Religious Ritual Behavior." Zygon 10, no. 1 (1975)

d'Aquili, Eugene. "The Myth-Ritual Complex: A Biogenetic Structural Analysis." Zygon 18, no. 3 (1983) d'Aquili, Eugene, and Andrew Newberg. The Mystical Mind: Probing the Biology of Religious Experience. Minneapolis: Fortress Press, 1999.

Daly DD. 1958. Ictal affect. Am J Psychiatry.

Damasio, A. (1994) Descartes' Error: Emotion, Reason and the Human Brain. New York, Putnams.

Damasio, A. (1999) The Feeling of What Happens: Body, Emotion and the Making of Consciousness. London, Heinemann.

Darwin, C. (1859) On the Origin of Species by Means of Natural Selection. London, Murray.

Darwin, C. (1871) The Descent of Man and Selection in Relation to Sex. London, John Murray.

Darwin, C. (1872) The Expression of the Emotions in Man and Animals. London, John Murray; also published

1965, Chicago, University of Chicago Press.

Dawkins, M.S. (1987) Minding and mattering. In C. Blakemore and S. Greenfield (eds) Mindwaves. Oxford, Blackwell, 151-60.

Dawkins, R. (1976) The Selfish Gene. Oxford, Oxford University Press; a new edition, with additional material, was published in 1989.

Dawkins, R. (1986) The Blind Watchmaker. London, Longman.

Di Pellegrino G, Fadiga L, Fogassi L, Gallese V, Rizzolatti G (1992) Understanding motor events: A neurophysiological study. Exp Brain Res 91: 176–80.

Deikman, A.J. (2000) A functional approach to mysticism. Journal of Consciousness Studies 7(11-12), 75-91.

Delmonte, M.M. (1987) Personality and meditation. In M. West (ed.) The

Psychology of Meditation. Oxford, Clarendon Press, 118-32.

Dennett, D.C. (1987) The Intentional Stance. Cambridge, MA, MIT Press.

Dennett, D.C. (1988) Quining qualia. In A.J. Marcel and E. Bisiach (eds) Consciousness in Contemporary Science. Oxford, Oxford University Press, 42-77.

Dennett, D.C. (1991) Consciousness Explained. Boston, MA, and London, Little, Brown and Co.

Dennett, D.C. (1995a) Darwin's Dangerous Idea. London, Penguin.

Dennett, D.C. (1995b) The unimagined preposterousness of zombies. Journal of Consciousness Studies 2(4), 322-6.

Dennett, D.C. (1995c) Cog: steps towards consciousness in robots. In T. Metzinger (ed.) Conscious Experience. Thorverton, Devon, Imprint Academic, 471-87.

Dennett, D.C. (1995d) The path not taken. Behavioral and Brain Sciences 18, 252-3; commentary on N. Block, On a confusion about a function of consciousness. Behavioral and Brain Sciences 18, 227.

Dennett, D.C. (1996a) Facing backwards on the problem of consciousness. Journal of Consciousness Studies 3(1), 4-6.

Dennett, D.C. (1996b) Kinds of Minds: Towards an Understanding of Consciousness. London, Weidenfeld & Nicolson.

Dennett, D.C. (1997) An exchange with Daniel Dennett. In J. Searle (ed.) The Mystery of Consciousness. New York, New York Review of Books, 115-19.

Dennett, D.C. (1998) The myth of double transduction. In S.R. Hameroff, A.W. Kaszniak and A. C. Scott (eds) Toward a Science of Consciousness: The Second Tucson Discussions and

Debates. Cambridge, MA, MIT Press, 97-107.

Dennett, D.C. (1998b) Brainchildren: Essays on Designing Minds. Cambridge, MA, MIT Press.

Dennett, D.C. (2001) The fantasy of first person science. Debate with D. Chalmers, Northwestern University, Evanston, IL, February 2001.

Dennett, D.C. (2003) Freedom Evolves. New York, Penguin.

Dennett, D.C. and Kinsbourne, M. (1992) Time and the observer: the where and when of consciousness in the brain. Behavioral and Brain Sciences 15, 183-247, including commentaries and authors' responses.

Dewey J., (1911 [1977]), "Epistemological Realism: The Alleged Ubiquity of the Knowledge Relation." Journal of Philosophy, VIII, 20 (September 28, 1911).

Dewhurst, Kenneth, and A. W. Beard. "Sudden Religious Conversions in Temporal Lobe Epilepsy." British Journal of Psychiatry 117 (1970)

Dewhurst K, Beard AW. Sudden religious conversions in temporal lobe epilepsy. 1970 Epilepsy Behav 2003

Devinsky O, Lai G. Spirituality and religion in epilepsy. Epilepsy Behav 2008.

Devinsky, O., Morrell, MJ, Vogt, BA. (1995) 'Contribution of anterior cingulate cortex to behavior', Brain, 118.

Douglas Stone A., Chapter 24, The Indian Comet, in the book Einstein and the Quantum, Princeton University Press, Princeton, New Jersey, 2013.

E. Horvitz, "One Hundred Year Study on Artificial Intelligence: Reflections and Framing," ed: Stanford University, 2014.

Einstein A. (1925). "Quantentheorie des einatomigen idealen Gases". Sitzungsberichte der Preussischen Akademie der Wissenschaften.

Eckhart Meister, Selected Writings

Egidi R., ed. (1999), "Von Wright and 'Dante's Dream': Stages in a Philosophical Pilgrim's Progress", in In Search of a New Humanism: the Philosophy of G.H. von Wright, ed. by R. Egidi, Kluwer, Dordrecht.

Fadiga L, Fogassi L, Pavesi G, Rizzolatti G (1995) Motor facilitation during action observation: a magnetic stimulation study. J Neurophysiol 73: 2608–2611.

Fogassi L, Gallese V, Fadiga L, Rizzolatti G (1998) Neurons responding to the sight of goal directed hand/arm actions in the parietal area PF (7b) of the macaque monkey. Soc Neurosci Abs 24:257.5.

Frith U, Frith CD (2003) Development and neurophysiology of mentalizing. Philos Trans R Soc Lond B Biol Sci 358: 459.

Farah, M.J. (1989), 'The neural basis of mental imagery', Trends in Neurosciences, 10.

Finlay BL, Darlington RB (1995) Linked regularities in the development and evolution of mammalian brains. Science 268.

Freud, S. "The Interpretation of Dreams", 1900

Freud, S. "Selected papers on hysteria and other psychoneuroses" Journal of Nervous and Mental Disease 1909.

Freud, S. "The Origin and Development of Psychoanalysis", 1910

Freud, S. "Psychopathology of everyday life", 1914

Freud, S. "Beyond the Pleasure Principle", 1920

Frith, C.D. & Dolan, R.J. (1997), 'Abnormal beliefs: Delusions and memory', Paper presented at the May, 1997, Harvard Conference on Memory and Belief.

Gay, Volney, ed. Neuroscience and Religion. Plymouth, UK: Lexington Books, 2009.

Gazzaniga, M. S. (1985). The social brain. New York: Basic Books.

Gazzaniga, M.S. (1993), 'Brain mechanisms and conscious experience', Ciba Foundation Symposium, 174.

Geschwind N. "Behavioural changes in temporal lobe epilepsy". Psychol Med. 1979.

Gellhorn, E., Kiely, W.F. "Mystical states of consciousness: neurophysiological and clinical aspects." J Nerv Ment Dis. 1972;154:399-405.

Gilbert SL, Dobyns WB, Lahn BT (2005) Genetic links between brain development and brain evolution. Nat Rev Genet 6.

Gray JA. The Psychology of Fear and Stress. 2nd ed. New York, NY: Cambridge University Press; 1988.

Gloor, P. (1992), 'Amygdala and temporal lobe epilepsy', in The Amygdala: Neurobiological Aspects of Emotion, Memory and Mental Dysfunction, ed J.P. Aggleton (New York: Wiley-Liss).

Greenspan, S. I. and S. G. Shanker (2004). The first idea: How symbols, language, and intelligence evolved from our early primate ancestors to modern humans. Cambridge, MA: Da Capo Press.

Grady, D. (1993), 'The vision thing: Mainly in the brain', Discover, June.

Gallagher HL, Frith CD (2003) Functional imaging of 'theory of mind'. Trends Cogn Sci 7: 77.

Gallese V, Fogassi L, Fadiga L, Rizzolatti G (2002) Action representation and the inferior parietal lobule. In: Prinz W, Hommel B (eds) Attention & Performance XIX. Common mechanisms in perception and action. Oxford University Press, Oxford.

Gallese V, Keysers C, Rizzolatti G (2004) A unifying view of the basis of social cognition. Trends Cogn Sci 8: 396–403.

Gangitano M, Mottaghy FM, Pascual-Leone A (2001) Phase specific modulation of cortical motor output during movement observation. NeuroReport 12: 1489–1492.

Gangitano M, Mottaghy FM, Pascual-Leone A (2004) Modulation of premotor mirror neuron activity during observation of unpredictable grasping movements. Eur J Neurosci 20: 2193– 2202.

Goldman AI, Sripada CS (2004) Simulationist models of face-based emotion recognition. Cognition 94: 193–213.

Grèzes J, Costes N, Decety J (1998) Top-down effect of strategy on the perception of human biological motion: a PET investigation. Cogn Neuropsychol 15: 553–582.

Grèzes J, Armony JL, Rowe J, Passingham RE (2003) Activations related to "mirror" and "canonical" neurones in the human brain: an fMRI study. Neuroimage 18: 928–937.

Gross CG, Rocha-Miranda CE, Bender DB (1972) Visual properties of neurons in the inferotemporal cortex of the macaque. J Neurophysiol 35: 96–111.

Hari R, Forss N, Avikainen S, Kirveskari S, Salenius S, Rizzolatti G

(1998) Activation of human primary motor cortex during action observation: a neuromagnetic study. Proc. Natl Acad Sci USA 95: 15061–15065.

Hardy, G. H. (1940). Ramanujan. Cambridge: Cambridge University Press.

Hall, Daniel, Keith Meador, and Harold Koenig. "Measuring Religiousness in Health Research: Review and Critique." Journal of Religion and Health 47, no. 2 (2008)

Harris, Sam, Jonas Kaplan, Ashley Curiel, Susan Bookheimer, Marco Iacoboni, and Mark Cohen. "The Neural Correlates of Religious and Nonreligious Belief." PLoS One 4, no. 10 (October 1, 2009)

Halgren, E. (1992), 'Emotional neurophysiology of the amygdala within the context of human cognition', in The Amygdala:

Neurobiological Aspects of Emotion, Memory and Mental Dysfunction, ed J.P. Aggleton (New York: Wiley-Liss).

Halligan PW, Fink GR, Marshal JC, Vallar G. 2003. Spatial cognition: evidence from visual neglect. Trends Cogn Sci.

Handbook of Emotions, Edited by Michael Lewis, Jeannette M. Haviland-Jones, and Lisa Feldman Barrett, The Guilford Press; 3rd edition (2010).

Haggard, P., Clark, S. and Kalogeras,]. (2002) Voluntary action and conscious awareness, Nature Neuroscience 5, 382-5. Haggard, P., Newman, C. and Magno, E. (1999) On the perceived time of voluntary actions. British Journal of Psychology 90, 291-303.

Hameroff, S.R. and Penrose, R. (1996) Conscious events as orchestrated space-time selections. Journal of Consciousness Studies 3(1), 36-53; also reprinted in J. Shear (ed.) (1997)

Explaining Consciousness-The Hard Problem. Cambridge, MA, MIT Press, 177-95.

Hardcastle, V.G. (2000) How to understand theN in NCC. InT. Metzinger (ed.) Neural Correlates of Consciousness. Cambridge, MA, MIT Press, 259-64.

Harding, D.E. (1961) On Having no Head: Zen and the Re-Discovery of the Obvious. London, Buddhist Society.

Hardy, A. (1979) The Spiritual Nature of Man: A Study of Contemporary Religious Experience. Oxford, Clarendon Press.

Hamad, S. (1990) The symbol grounding problem. Physica D 42, 335-46.

Hamad, S. (2001) No easy way out. The Sciences 41(2), 36-42.

Harre, R. and Gillett, G. (1994) The Discursive Mind. Thousand Oaks, CA, Sage.

Haugeland, J. (ed.) (1997) Mind Design II: Philosophy, Psychology, Artificial Intelligence. Cambridge, MA, MIT Press.

Hauser, M.D. (2000) Wild Minds: What Animals Really Think. New York, Henry Holt and Co.; London, Penguin.

Hearne, K. (1990) The Dream Machine. Northants, Aquarian.

Hebb, D.O. (1949) The Organization of Behavior. New York, Wiley.

Helmholtz, H.L.F. von (1856-67) Treatise on Physiological Optics.

Hess, EH (1975) "The role of pupil size in communication," Scientific American, 233(5), 110–12.

Heyes, C.M. (1998) Theory of mind in nonhuman primates. Behavioral and

Brain Sciences 21, 101-48; with commentaries.

Heyes, C.M. and Galef, B.G. (eds) (1996) Social Learning in Animals: The Roots of Culture. San Diego, CA, Academic Press.

Hilgard, E.R. (1986) Divided Consciousness: Multiple Controls in Human Thought and Action. New York, Wiley.

Hocquette JF (2016) Is in vitro meat the

solution for the future? Meat Science 120:

167–176

Hodgson, R. (1891) A case of double consciousness. Proceedings of the Society for Psychical Research 7, 221-58.

Hofstadter, D.R. (1979) Code!, Escher, Bach: An Eternal Golden Braid. London, Penguin.

Hofstadter, D.R. and Dennett, D.C. (eds) (1981) The Mind's I: Fantasies and Reflections on Self and Soul. London, Penguin.

Holland, J. (ed.) (2001) Ecstasy: The Complete Guide: A Comprehensive Look at the Risks and Benefits of MDMA. Rochester, VT, Park Street Press.

Holmes, D.S. (1987) The influence of meditation versus rest on physiological arousal. In M. West (ed.) The Psychology of Meditation. Oxford, Clarendon Press, 81-103.

Holt, J. (1999) Blindsight in debates about qualia. Journal of Consciousness Studies 6(5), 54-71.

Horgan, J. (1994), 'Can science explain consciousness?', Scientific American, 271.

Holloway RL (1996) Evolution of the human brain. In: Lock A, Peters CR (eds) Handbook of human symbolic evolution. Oxford University Press, Oxford

Iacoboni M, Woods RP, Brass M, Bekkering H, Mazziotta JC, Rizzolatti G (1999) Cortical mechanisms of human imitation. Science 286: 2526–2528.

Iacoboni M, Koski LM, Brass M, Bekkering H, Woods RP, Dubeau MC, Mazziotta JC, Rizzolatti G (2001) Reafferent copies of imitated actions in the right superior temporal cortex. Proc Natl Acad Sci USA 98: 13995–13999.

Jeannerod M (1988) The neural and behavioural organization of goal-directed movements. Clarendon Press, Oxford.

Johnson-Frey SH, Maloof FR, Newman-Norlund R, Farrer C, Inati S, Grafton ST (2003) Actions or hand-objects interactions? Human inferior frontal cortex and action observation. Neuron 39: 1053–1058.

Jackson, F. (1982) Epiphenomenal qualia. Philosophical Quarterly 32, 127-36.

James, W. (1890) The Principles of Psychology (2 volumes). London, Macmillan.

James, W. (1902) The Varieties of Religious Experience: A Study in Human Nature. New York and London, Longmans, Green and Co.

Jansen, K. (2001) Ketamine: Dreams and Realities. Sarasota, FL, Multidisciplinary Association for Psychedelic Studies.

Jay, M. (ed.) (1999) Artificial Paradises: A Drugs Reader. London, Penguin.

Jaynes, J. (1976) The Origin of Consciousness in the Breakdown of the Bicameral Mind. New York, Houghton Mifflin.

Johnson, M.K. and Raye, C.L. (1981) Reality monitoring. Psychological Review 88, 67-85.

Kadim I, Mahgoub O, Baqir S et al. (2015) Cultured meat from muscle stem cells: a review of challenges and prospects. J Integr Agr 14: 222–233

Koski L, Iacoboni M, Dubeau MC, Woods RP, Mazziotta JC (2003) Modulation of cortical activity during different imitative behaviors. J Neurophysiol 89: 460–471.

Krolak-Salmon P, Henaff MA, Isnard J, Tallon-Baudry C, Guenot M, Vighetto A, Bertrand O, Mauguiere F (2003) An attention modulated response to disgust in human ventral anterior insula. Ann Neurol 53: 446–453.

Kandel, E. R. In Search of Memory: The Emergence of a New Science of Mind, W. W. Norton & Company (2007).

Kandel E. R. Schwartz JH, Jessel TM. Principles of neural sciences. New York; McGraw Hill, 2000.

Kanizsa, G. (1979), Organization In Vision (New York: Praeger).

Kaloupek DG, Scott JR, Khatami V. Assessment of coping strategies associated with syncope in blood donors. J Psychosom Res. 1985;29:207-214.

Kanwisher, N. (2001) Neural events and perceptual awareness. Cognition 79, 89-113; also reprinted inS. Dehaene (ed.) The Cognitive Neuroscience of Consciousness. Cambridge, MA, MIT Press, 89-113.

Kapleau, Roshi P. (1980) The Three Pillars of Zen: Teaching, Practice, and Enlightenment (revised edn). New York, Doubleday.

Karn, K. and Hayhoe, M. (2000) Memory representations guide

targeting eye movements in a natural task. Visual Cognition 7, 673-703.

Kasamatsu, A. and Hirai, T. (1966) An electroencephalographic study on the Zen meditation (zazen). Folia Psychiatrica et Neurologica Japonica 20, 315-36.

Kaiserman-Abramof, I. R., Graybiel, A. M., & Nauta, W. J. (1980). The thalamic projection to cortical area 17 in a congenitally anophthalmic mouse strain. Neuroscience, 5, 41–52.

Kanold, P. O., Kara, P., Reid, R. C., & Shatz, C. J. (2003). Role of subplate neurons in functional maturation of visual cortical columns. Science, 301, 521–525.

Kennedy, H., & Dehay, C. (1988). Functional implications of the anatomical organization of the callosal projections of visual areas V1 and V2 in the macaque monkey. Behav. Brain Res., 29, 225–236.

Kentridge, R.W. and Heywood, C.A. (1999) The status of blindsight. Journal of Consciousness Studies 6(5), 3-11.

Kihlstrom, J.F. (1996) Perception without awareness of what is perceived, learning without awareness of what is learned. In M. Velmans (ed.) The Science of Consciousness. London, Routledge, 23-46.

Kollerstrom, N. (1999) The path of Halley's comet, and Newton's late apprehension of the law of gravity. Annals of Science 56, 331-56.

Kosslyn, S.M. (1980) Image and Mind. Cambridge, MA, Harvard University Press.

Kosslyn, S.M. (1988) Aspects of a cognitive neuroscience of mental imagery. Science 240, 1621-6.

Kinsbourne, M. (1995), 'The intralaminar thalamic nucleii', Consciousness and Cognition, 4.

Kjaer, Troels, Camilla Bertelsen, Paola Piccini, David Brooks, Jorgen Alving, and Hans Lou. "Increased Dopamine Tone during Meditation- Induced Change of Consciousness." Cognitive Brain Research 13, no. 2 (April 2002)

Kölmel HW. 1985. Complex visual hallucinations in the hemianopic field. J Neurol Neurosurg Psychiatry.

Koenig, Harold. "Research on Religion, Spirituality, and Mental Health: A Review." Canadian Journal of Psychiatry 54, no. 5 (May 2009)

Koenig, Harold, ed. Handbook of Religion and Mental Health. San Diego, CA: Academic Press, 1998

Kraepelin E. Psychiatry: A Textbook for Students and Physicians. New York, NY: Science History Publications; 1990.

Lauglin, Charles, John McManus, and Eugene d'Aquili. Brain, Symbol, and

Experience. 2nd ed. New York: Columbia University Press, 1992

Lakoff, G. and M. Johnson (1999). Philosophy in the flesh. Basic Books: New York.

LeDoux, J. E. (1996). The emotional brain. New York: Simon & Schuster.

LeDoux, J.E. (1992), 'Emotion and the amygdala', in The Amygdala: Neurobiological Aspects of Emo- tion, Memory and Mental Dysfunction, ed J.P. Aggleton (New York: Wiley-Liss).

Levin, D.T. and Simons, D.J. (1997) Failure to detect changes to attended objects in motion pictures. Psychonomic Bulletin and Review 4, 501-6.

Levine,J. (1983) Materialism and qualia: the explanatory gap. Pacific Philosophical Quarterly 64, 354-61.

Levine,J. (2001) Purple Haze: The Puzzle of Consciousness. New York,

Oxford University Press. Levine, S. (1979) A Gradual Awakening. New York, Doubleday.

Levinson, B.W. (1965) States of awareness during general anaesthesia. British Journal of Anaesthesia 37, 544-6.

Lewicki, P., Czyzewska, M. and Hoffman, H. (1987) Unconscious acquisition of complex procedural knowledge. Journal of Experimental Psychology: Learning, Memory and Cognition 13, 523-30.

Lewicki, P., Hill, T. and Bizot, E. (1988) Acquisition of procedural knowledge about a pattern of stimuli that cannot be articulated. Cognitive Psychology 20, 24-37.

Lewicki, P., Hill, T. and Czyzewska, M. (1992) Nonconscious acquisition of information. American Psychologist 47, 796-801.

Manthey S, Schubotz RI, von Cramon DY (2003). Premotor cortex in observing erroneous action: an fMRI study. Brain Res Cogn Brain Res 15: 296–307.

Mesulam MM, Mufson EJ (1982) Insula of the old world monkey. III: Efferent cortical output and comments on function. J Comp Neurol 212: 38–52.

Naskar, Abhijit. "Homo: A Brief History of Consciousness", 2015

Naskar, Abhijit. "What is Mind?", 2016

Naskar, Abhijit. "In Search of Divinity: Journey to The Kingdom of Conscience", 2016

Naskar, Abhijit. "Love, God & Neurons: Memoir of A Scientist who found himself by getting lost", 2016

Naskar, Abhijit. "Neurons of Jesus: Mind of A Teacher, Spouse & Thinker", 2017

Naskar, Abhijit. "The Islamophobic Civilization: Voyage of Acceptance", 2017

Naskar, Abhijit. "Principia Humanitas", 2017

Naskar, Abhijit. "We Are All Black: A Treatise on Racism", 2017

Naskar, Abhijit. "Wise Mating: A Treatise on Monogamy", 2017

Naskar, Abhijit. "Illusion of Religion: A Treatise on Religious Fundamentalism", 2017

Naskar, Abhijit. "I Am The Thread: My Mission", 2017

Naskar, Abhijit. "The Bengal Tigress: A Treatise on Gender Equality", 2017

Naskar, Abhijit. "Morality Absolute", 2017

Naskar, Abhijit. "Build Bridges not Walls: In the name of Americana", 2018

Naskar, Abhijit. "Fabric of Humanity", 2018

Naskar, Abhijit. "Lives To Serve Before I Sleep", 2019

Naskar, Abhijit. "Citizens of Peace: Beyond the Savagery of Sovereignty", 2019

Naskar, Abhijit. "The Constitution of The United Peoples of Earth", 2019

Naskar, Abhijit. "Neurons Giveth, Neurons Taketh Away | Abhijit Naskar | TEDxIIMRanchi", 2019 https://www.youtube.com/watch?v=B NX-Q0ySm80

Naskar, Abhijit. "Mission Reality", 2019

Naskar, Abhijit. "Operation Justice: To Make A Society That Needs No Law", 2019

Naskar, Abhijit. "Every Generation Needs Caretakers: The Gospel of Patriotism", 2020

Newberg, Andrew, and Jeremy Iversen. "The Neural Basis of the Complex Mental Task of Meditation: Neurotransmitter and Neurochemical Considerations." Medical Hypotheses 61, no. 2 (2003).

Newberg, Andrew. "How God Changes Your Brain: An Introduction to Jewish Neurotheology", CCAR Journal: The Reform Jewish Quarterly, Winter 2016.

Newberg, Andrew, and Stephanie Newberg. "A Neuropsychological Perspective on Spiritual Development." In Handbook of Spiritual Development in Childhood and Adolescence, edited by Eugene Roehlkepartain, Pamela King, Linda Wagener, and Peter Benson. London: Sage Publications, Inc., 2005

Newberg, Andrew. "The Neurotheology Link An Intersection Between Spirituality and Health",

Alternative and Complimentary Therapies, Vol 21 No 1, February 2015.

Newberg, Andrew, Nancy Wintering, Dharma Khalsa, Hannah Roggenkamp, and Mark Waldman. "Meditation Effects on Cognitive Function and Cerebral Blood Flow in Subjects with Memory Loss: A Preliminary Study." Journal of Alzheimer's Disease 20, no. 2 (2010)

Nash, M. (1995), 'Glimpses of the mind', Time.

Nesse RM. Proximate and evolutionary studies of anxiety, stress and depression: synergy at the interface. Neurosci Biobehav Rev. 1999;23:895-903.

Nicolelis, Miguel. (2011) "Beyond Boundaries: The New Neuroscience of Connecting Brains with Machines---and How It Will Change Our Lives", Times Books

O'Hara, K. and Scutt, T. (1996) There is no hard problem of consciousness. Journal of Consciousness Studies 3(4), 290-302, reprinted in J. Shear (ed.) (1997) Explaining Consciousness. Cambridge, MA, MIT Press, 69-82.

O'Regan, J.K. (1992) Solving the "real" mysteries of visual perception: the world as an outside memory. Canadian Journal of Psychology 46, 461-88.

O'Regan, J.K. and Noe, A. (2001) A sensorimotor account of vision and visual consciousness. Behavioral and Brain Sciences 24(5), 883-917.

O'Regan, J.K., Rensink, R.A. and Clark,].]. (1999) Change-blindness as a result of "mudsplashes." Nature 398, 34.

Ornstein, R.E. (1977) The Psychology of Consciousness (2nd edn). New York, Harcourt.

Ornstein, R.E. (1986) The Psychology of Consciousness (3rd edn). New York, Pehguin.

Ornstein, R.E. (1992) The Evolution of Consciousness. New York, Touchstone.

Penfield W, Faulk ME (1955) The insula: further observations on its function. Brain 78: 445– 470.

Penrose, R. (1994), Shadows of the Mind (Oxford: Oxford University Press).

Penrose, R. (1989), The Emperor's New Mind: Concerning Computers, Minds and The Laws of Physics (Oxford: Oxford University Press).

Persinger, "'I would kill in God's name' role of sex, weekly church attendance, report of a religious experience and limbic lability" Perceptual and Motor Skills 1997.

Persinger "Experimental simulation of the God experience" Neurotheology 2003.

Persinger, M. A. (1993b). Personality changes following brain injury as a grief response to the loss of sense of self: Phenomenological themes as indices of local lability and neurocognitive restructuring as psycho- therapy. Psychological Reports, 72

Persinger, Corradini, Clement, Keaney, et al "Neurotheology and its convergence with neuroquantology" NeuroQuantology 2010.

Persinger, Koren and St-Pierre "The electromagnetic induction of mystical and altered states within the laboratory" Journal of Consciousness Exploration and Research 2010.

Persinger "Case report: A prototypical spontaneous 'sensed presence' of a sentient being and concomitant electroencephalographic activity in the clinical laboratory" Neurocase 2008.

Persinger and Saroka "Potential production of Hughlings Jackson's "parasitic consciousness" by physiologically-patterned weak transcerebral magnetic fields: QEEG and source localization" Epilepsy & Behavior 28 (2013).

Persinger. "The neuropsychiatry of paranormal experiences". J Neuropsychiatry Clin Neurosci 2001.

Persinger. "Neuropsychological bases of god beliefs", New York: Praeger, 1987

Persinger. "Temporal lobe epileptic signs and correlative behaviors displayed by normal populations", Journal of General Psychology, 1986

Perry BD, Pollard R. Homeostasis, stress, trauma, and adaptation. A neurodevelopmental view of childhood trauma. Child Adolesc Psychiatr Clin N Am. 1998;7:33.

Paré, D. & Llinás, R. (1995), 'Conscious and preconscious processes as seen from the standpoint of sleep-waking cycle neurophysiology', Neuropsychologia, 33.

P. S. de Laplace. Essai Philosophique sur les Probabilites [1814], in Academy des Sciences, Oeuvres Complotes de Laplace, Vol. 7, Gauthier-Villars, Paris (1886).

Perrett DI, Harries MH, Bevan R, Thomas S, Benson PJ, Mistlin AJ, Chitty AJ, Hietanen JK, Ortega JE (1989) Frameworks of analysis for the neural representation of animate objects and actions. J Exp Bio 146: 87–113.

Phillips ML, Young AW, Senior C, Brammer M, Andrew C, Calder AJ, Bullmore ET, Perrett DI, Rowland D, Williams SC, Gray JA, David AS (1997)

A specific neural substrate for perceiving facial expressions of disgust. Nature 389: 495–498.

Phillips ML, Young AW, Scott SK, Calder AJ, Andrew C, Giampietro V, Williams SC, Bullmore ET, Brammer M, Gray JA (1998) Neural responses to facial and vocal expressions of fear and disgust. Proc R Soc Lond B Biol Sci 265: 1809–1817.

Puce A, Perrett D (2003) Electrophysiological and brain imaging of biological motion. Philosoph Trans Royal Soc Lond, Series B, 358: 435–445.

Ramachandran VS. Behavioral and magnetoencephalographic correlates of plasticity in the adult human brain. Proc Natl Acad Sci USA 1993; 90: 10413–20.

Ramachandran VS. Phantom limbs, neglect syndromes, repressed memories, and Freudian psychology. Int Rev Neurobiol 1994; 37: 291–333.

Ramachandran VS. Plasticity and functional recovery in neurology. Clin Med 2005; 5: 368–73.

Ramachandran VS, Hirstein W. The perception of phantom limbs. The D. O. Hebb lecture. Brain 1998; 121: 1603–30.

Ramachandran VS, Rogers-Ramachandran D, Cobb S. Touching the phantom limb. Nature 1995; 377: 489–90.

Ramachandran VS, Rogers-Ramachandran D. Phantom limbs and neural plasticity. Arch Neurol 2000; 57: 317–20.

Ramachandran VS, Rogers-Ramachandran D. It's all done with mirrors. Sci Am Mind 2007; 18: 16–9.

Ramachandran VS, Rogers-Ramachandran D. Sensations referred

to a patient's phantom arm from another subjects intact arm: perceptual correlates of mirror neurons. Med Hypotheses 2008; 70: 1233–4.

Ramachandran VS, Rogers-Ramachandran D, Stewart M. Perceptual correlates of massive cortical reorganization. Science 1992; 258: 1159–60.

Rizzolatti G, Craighero L (2004) The mirror-neuron system. Annu Rev Neurosci 27: 169–192.

Rizzolatti G, Fogassi L, Gallese V (2001) Neurophysiological mechanisms underlying the understanding and imitation of action. Nature Rev Neurosci 2:661–670.

Rock I, Victor J. Vision and touch: an experimentally created conflict between the two senses. Science 1964; 143: 594–6.

Rose'n B, Lundborg G. Training with a mirror in rehabilitation of the hand.

Scand J Plast Reconstr Surg Hand Surg 2005; 39: 104–8.

Royet JP, Plailly J, Delon-Martin C, Kareken DA, Segebarth C (2003) fMRI of emotional responses to odors: influence of hedonic valence and judgment, handedness, and gender. Neuroimage 20: 713–728.

Rozin R Haidt J and McCauley CR (2000) Disgust. In: Lewis M, Haviland-Jones JM (eds) Handbook of Emotion. 2nd Edition. Guilford Press, New York, pp 637–653.

Saxe R, Carey S, Kanwisher N (2004) Understanding other minds: linking developmental psychology and functional neuroimaging. Annu Rev Psychol 55: 87–124.

S. J. Russell and P. Norvig, Artificial intelligence: a modern approach (3rd edition): Prentice Hall, 2009.

Schienle A, Stark R, Walter B, Blecker C, Ott U, Kirsch P, Sammer G, Vaitl D

(2002) The insula is not specifically involved in disgust processing: an fMRI study. Neuroreport 13: 2023–2026.

Showers MJC, Lauer EW (1961) Somatovisceral motor patterns in the insula. J Comp Neurol 117: 107–115.

Singer T, Seymour B, O'Doherty J, Kaube H, Dolan RJ, Frith CD (2004) Empathy for pain involves the affective but not the sensory components of pain. Science 303: 1157–1162.

Smith A (1759) The theory of moral sentiments (ed. 1976). Clarendon Press, Oxford.

S. N. Bose (1924). "Plancks Gesetz und Lichtquantenhypothese". Zeitschrift für Physik. 26 (1): 178–181.

Sprengelmeyer R, Rausch M, Eysel UT, Przuntek H (1998) Neural structures associated with recognition of facial expressions of basic emotions Proc R Soc Lond B Biol Sci 265: 1927–1931.

Strafella AP, Paus T (2000) Modulation of cortical excitability during action observation: a transcranial magnetic stimulation study. NeuroReport 11: 2289–2292.

Simonsen R (2015) Eating for the future: veganism and the challenge of in vitro meat. In: Stapleton P, Byers A (Hg). Biopolitics and utopia. Palgrave Macmillan, New York (2015), S 167–190

Tanaka K (1996) Inferotemporal cortex and object vision. Ann Rev Neurosci. 19: 109–140.

Tesla N. "My Inventions", 1919

T. R. Society, "Machine learning: the power and promise of computers that learn by example," ed. The Royal Society, 2017.

Tomasello M, Call J (1997) Primate cognition. Oxford University Press, Oxford.

Tremblay C, Robert M, Pascual-Leone A, Lepore F, Nguyen DK, Carmant L, Bouthillier A, Theoret H (2004) Action observation and execution: intracranial recordings in a human subject. Neurology. 63: 937–938.

Umilta MA, Kohler E, Gallese V, Fogassi L, Fadiga L, Keysers C, Rizzolatti G (2001) "I know what you are doing": a neurophysiological study. Neuron 32: 91–101.

Von Wright G.H., (1963), Norm and Action. A Logical Inquiry, Routledge & Kegan Paul, London.

Von Wright G.H., (1976), "Determinism and the Study of Man", in Essays on Explanation and Understanding, ed. by J. Manninen and R. Tuomela, Reidel, Dordrecht.

Von Wright G.H., (1977), "What is Humanism?", The Lindlay Lecture, University of Arkansas, Lawrence, Kansas.

Von Wright G.H., (1979), "Humanism and the Humanities", in Philosophy and Grammar, ed. by S. Kanger and S. Öhman, Reidel, Dordrecht, pp. 1-16. Reprinted in von Wright (1993).

Von Wright G.H., (1980), Freedom and Determination, North-Holland Publishing Co., Amsterdam.

Von Wright G.H., (1985), Of Human Freedom, The Tanner Lectures on Human Values,

Vol. VI, ed. by S. M. McMurrin, University of Utah Press, Salt Lake City, pp. 107-70. Reprinted in von Wright (1998).

Von Wright G.H., (1993), The Tree of Knowledge and Other Essays, Brill, Leiden.

Von Wright G.H., (1997), "Progress: Fact and Fiction", in The Idea of Progress, ed. by A. Burgen et al., W. de Gruyter, Berlin, pp. 1-18.

Von Wright G.H., (1998), In the Shadow of Descartes: Essays in the Philosophy of Mind, Kluwer, Dordrecht.